A
Name
Above
All Others

Journal

MaryAnn Ward

ReMade Ministries
Regina, SK

Copyright

MaryAnn Ward Copyright 2022

All rights reserved.

ISBN - 978-1-7771316-8-5

**Published in Canada by
ReMade Ministries
Regina, SK S4V 3G5**

Digitally printed in Canada by

PAGEMASTER
PUBLISHING
PageMasterPublishing.ca

Introduction

"This is the covenant I will establish . . .
after that time, declares the Lord.
I will put my laws in their minds
and write them on their hearts.
I will be their God,
and they will be my people.
No longer will they teach their neighbor,
or say to one another, 'Know the Lord,'
because they will all know me,
from the least of them to the greatest."
Hebrews 8:10-11

A Name Above All Others Journal practically applies the **S-T-E-P** devotional principle of **Scripture**, **Take Away, Early**, and **Prayer** to help progressively guide into a deeper, more vibrant, and fulfilled spiritual life.

To *know* in this verse means "to grow in knowledge of and to come to know personally." The second *know*, has a meaning of "to perceive to know absolutely, a complete knowledge of.

Because of the immensity of God, completely knowing Him will become our eternal endeavor, seeing, discovering and knowing Him in ever-increasing ways. May you experience God in powerful ways as you consider the vastness of His character and nature expressed through His names.

Genesis 1:1-2   *Creator — Elohim*

Scripture
Write out the Scripture.

Take Away
What key point(s) did you find in this Scripture and devotion?

Early 1.
How might knowing this Name for God impact my daily life?

Early 2.
How might knowing God more in this way help me grow spiritually?

Prayer
Write or doodle your prayer.

Judges 6:24   *The LORD is Peace — Jehovah-Shalom*

Scripture
Write out the Scripture.

Take Away
What key point(s) did you find in this Scripture and devotion?

Early 1.
How might knowing this Name for God impact my daily life?

Early 2.
How might knowing God more in this way help me grow spiritually?

Prayer

Write or doodle your prayer.

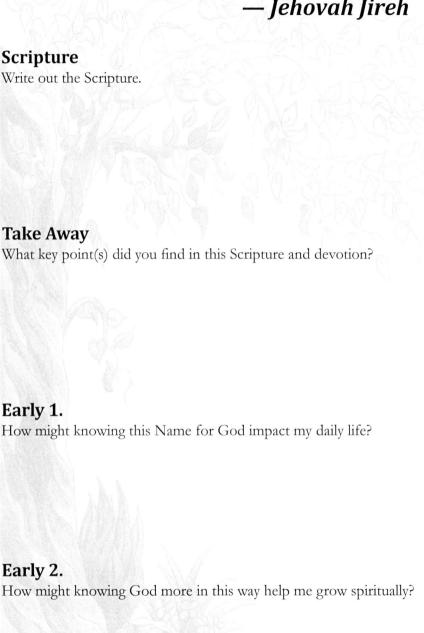

Philippians 4:19 — *The LORD Who Provides — Jehovah Jireh*

Scripture
Write out the Scripture.

Take Away
What key point(s) did you find in this Scripture and devotion?

Early 1.
How might knowing this Name for God impact my daily life?

Early 2.
How might knowing God more in this way help me grow spiritually?

Prayer

Write or doodle your prayer.

1 Corinthians 15:57

The LORD My Banner — Jehovah Nissi

Scripture
Write out the Scripture.

Take Away
What key point(s) did you find in this Scripture and devotion?

Early 1.
How might knowing this Name for God impact my daily life?

Early 2.
How might knowing God more in this way help me grow spiritually?

Prayer

Write or doodle your prayer.

1 Timothy 6: 15b-16　　　*King of Kings*

Scripture
Write out the Scripture.

Take Away
What key point(s) did you find in this Scripture and devotion?

Early 1.
How might knowing this Name for God impact my daily life?

Early 2.
How might knowing God more in this way help me grow spiritually?

Prayer

Write or doodle your prayer.

1 Peter 2:6-7 *The Cornerstone*

Scripture
Write out the Scripture.

Take Away
What key point(s) did you find in this Scripture and devotion?

Early 1.
How might knowing this Name for God impact my daily life?

Early 2.
How might knowing God more in this way help me grow spiritually?

Prayer
Write or doodle your prayer.

Exodus 3:14   *I AM WHO I AM*

Scripture
Write out the Scripture.

Take Away
What key point(s) did you find in this Scripture and devotion?

Early 1.
How might knowing this Name for God impact my daily life?

Early 2.
How might knowing God more in this way help me grow spiritually?

Prayer

Write or doodle your prayer.

John 14:6   *The Way*

Scripture
Write out the Scripture.

Take Away
What key point(s) did you find in this Scripture and devotion?

Early 1.
How might knowing this Name for God impact my daily life?

Early 2.
How might knowing God more in this way help me grow spiritually?

Prayer

Write or doodle your prayer.

Psalm 18:2   *A Strong Tower*

Scripture
Write out the Scripture.

Take Away
What key point(s) did you find in this Scripture and devotion?

Early 1.
How might knowing this Name for God impact my daily life?

Early 2.
How might knowing God more in this way help me grow spiritually?

Prayer
Write or doodle your prayer.

Psalm 90:1-2   *Everlasting God*
— El Olam

Scripture
Write out the Scripture.

Take Away
What key point(s) did you find in this Scripture and devotion?

Early 1.
How might knowing this Name for God impact my daily life?

Early 2.
How might knowing God more in this way help me grow spiritually?

Prayer

Write or doodle your prayer.

Revelation 22: 16-17

Bright Morning Star

Scripture
Write out the Scripture.

Take Away
What key point(s) did you find in this Scripture and devotion?

Early 1.
How might knowing this Name for God impact my daily life?

Early 2.
How might knowing God more in this way help me grow spiritually?

Prayer

Write or doodle your prayer.

John 5:25-26   *The Giver of Life*

Scripture
Write out the Scripture.

Take Away
What key point(s) did you find in this Scripture and devotion?

Early 1.
How might knowing this Name for God impact my daily life?

Early 2.
How might knowing God more in this way help me grow spiritually?

Prayer

Write or doodle your prayer.

2 Corinthians 1: 3-4

Comforter

Scripture
Write out the Scripture.

Take Away
What key point(s) did you find in this Scripture and devotion?

Early 1.
How might knowing this Name for God impact my daily life?

Early 2.
How might knowing God more in this way help me grow spiritually?

Prayer
Write or doodle your prayer.

1 Timothy 1:15   *Friend of Sinners*

Scripture
Write out the Scripture.

Take Away
What key point(s) did you find in this Scripture and devotion?

Early 1.
How might knowing this Name for God impact my daily life?

Early 2.
How might knowing God more in this way help me grow spiritually?

Prayer

Write or doodle your prayer.

Psalm 23:1   *The LORD is My Shepherd*
— Jehovah Roi

Scripture
Write out the Scripture.

Take Away
What key point(s) did you find in this Scripture and devotion?

Early 1.
How might knowing this Name for God impact my daily life?

Early 2.
How might knowing God more in this way help me grow spiritually?

Prayer

Write or doodle your prayer.

John 3:1-2   *Good Teacher*

Scripture
Write out the Scripture.

Take Away
What key point(s) did you find in this Scripture and devotion?

Early 1.
How might knowing this Name for God impact my daily life?

Early 2.
How might knowing God more in this way help me grow spiritually?

Prayer
Write or doodle your prayer.

Mark 10:45   *Servant*

Scripture
Write out the Scripture.

Take Away
What key point(s) did you find in this Scripture and devotion?

Early 1.
How might knowing this Name for God impact my daily life?

Early 2.
How might knowing God more in this way help me grow spiritually?

Prayer

Write or doodle your prayer.

Revelation 5:5   *The Lion of the Tribe of Judah*

Scripture
Write out the Scripture.

Take Away
What key point(s) did you find in this Scripture and devotion?

Early 1.
How might knowing this Name for God impact my daily life?

Early 2.
How might knowing God more in this way help me grow spiritually?

Prayer
Write or doodle your prayer.

John 14:7-9   *Our Father*

Scripture
Write out the Scripture.

Take Away
What key point(s) did you find in this Scripture and devotion?

Early 1.
How might knowing this Name for God impact my daily life?

Early 2.
How might knowing God more in this way help me grow spiritually?

Prayer

Write or doodle your prayer.

Psalm 27:1 — *Light of the World*

Scripture
Write out the Scripture.

Take Away
What key point(s) did you find in this Scripture and devotion?

Early 1.
How might knowing this Name for God impact my daily life?

Early 2.
How might knowing God more in this way help me grow spiritually?

Prayer

Write or doodle your prayer.

Isaiah 33:22   *Righteous Judge*

Scripture
Write out the Scripture.

Take Away
What key point(s) did you find in this Scripture and devotion?

Early 1.
How might knowing this Name for God impact my daily life?

Early 2.
How might knowing God more in this way help me grow spiritually?

Prayer
Write or doodle your prayer.

1 Peter 2:6   *A Chosen & Precious Cornerstone*

Scripture
Write out the Scripture.

Take Away
What key point(s) did you find in this Scripture and devotion?

Early 1.
How might knowing this Name for God impact my daily life?

Early 2.
How might knowing God more in this way help me grow spiritually?

Prayer

Write or doodle your prayer.

Psalm 46:7 KJV

The LORD of Hosts — Jehovah Sabaoth

Scripture
Write out the Scripture.

Take Away
What key point(s) did you find in this Scripture and devotion?

Early 1.
How might knowing this Name for God impact my daily life?

Early 2.
How might knowing God more in this way help me grow spiritually?

Prayer
Write or doodle your prayer.

Psalm 139:7-10 — *The God Who Sees — El Roi*

Scripture
Write out the Scripture.

Take Away
What key point(s) did you find in this Scripture and devotion?

Early 1.
How might knowing this Name for God impact my daily life?

Early 2.
How might knowing God more in this way help me grow spiritually?

Prayer
Write or doodle your prayer.

Philippians 2:9-11 *Jesus*

Scripture
Write out the Scripture.

Take Away
What key point(s) did you find in this Scripture and devotion?

Early 1.
How might knowing this Name for God impact my daily life?

Early 2.
How might knowing God more in this way help me grow spiritually?

Prayer
Write or doodle your prayer.

2 Corinthians 9:15　　　*Gift of God*

Scripture
Write out the Scripture.

Take Away
What key point(s) did you find in this Scripture and devotion?

Early 1.
How might knowing this Name for God impact my daily life?

Early 2.
How might knowing God more in this way help me grow spiritually?

Prayer

Write or doodle your prayer.

1 Corinthians 1:30   *The LORD Who Makes Holy*
NLT   *— Jehovah M'Kaddesh*

Scripture
Write out the Scripture.

Take Away
What key point(s) did you find in this Scripture and devotion?

Early 1.
How might knowing this Name for God impact my daily life?

Early 2.
How might knowing God more in this way help me grow spiritually?

Prayer

Write or doodle your prayer.

John 1:1   *The Word*

Scripture
Write out the Scripture.

Take Away
What key point(s) did you find in this Scripture and devotion?

Early 1.
How might knowing this Name for God impact my daily life?

Early 2.
How might knowing God more in this way help me grow spiritually?

Prayer
Write or doodle your prayer.

Romans 4:20-21   *Almighty God*
— El Shaddai

Scripture
Write out the Scripture.

Take Away
What key point(s) did you find in this Scripture and devotion?

Early 1.
How might knowing this Name for God impact my daily life?

Early 2.
How might knowing God more in this way help me grow spiritually?

Prayer

Write or doodle your prayer.

Psalm 28:7

The Lord My Strength & Shield

Scripture
Write out the Scripture.

Take Away
What key point(s) did you find in this Scripture and devotion?

Early 1.
How might knowing this Name for God impact my daily life?

Early 2.
How might knowing God more in this way help me grow spiritually?

Prayer
Write or doodle your prayer.

Luke 7:21   *The LORD Who Heals*
                     — Jehovah Rapha

Scripture
Write out the Scripture.

Take Away
What key point(s) did you find in this Scripture and devotion?

Early 1.
How might knowing this Name for God impact my daily life?

Early 2.
How might knowing God more in this way help me grow spiritually?

Prayer
Write or doodle your prayer.

Author Bio

Like people throughout the ages, the author's journey toward, and with, God continues to be a life-long process. MaryAnn means "bitter grace." These two aspects of life (the difficult and the gentle), that refine, test, and draw one into intimacy with the Father, have defined the author's life as well. In drinking from both sides of the cup, the bitter and the sweet, God has proved Himself sufficient in all seasons and for every need.

MaryAnn's teaching, speaking, and writing emanate from the rich resource of these life experiences and from extensive study of the Bible. MaryAnn encourages people of all ages in their pursuit of God, helping them live a fulfilling and satisfying spiritual life.

She fully acknowledges that every personal accomplishment and achievement belongs solely and ultimately to Jesus Christ. MaryAnn solemnly recognizes that all she is, or will ever be, she owes to Him. He alone receives any and all accolades.

"I am the vine; you are the branches.
If you remain in me and I in you,
you will bear much fruit;
apart from me you can do nothing."
John 15:5

Contact

Check out additional resources, blogs, and products here!

https://maward.ca/about-maryann-ward/

ReMade Ministries
407 - 2885 Arens Rd E.
Regina, Saskatchewan, CA
S4V 3G5

maryann@maward.ca

Email signup right here!

Companion Book

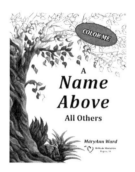

A Name Above All Others Coloring Book includes inspirational devotionals with corresponding coloring pages, Bible verses and prayers A bonus full color section contains a comprehensive list of the Names of God. *A Name Above All Others* will help develop an increased appreciation of God's greatness, a deepened understanding of God's nature, apersonal encouragement and hope.

Published 2022: Purchase and Review at

- Amazon.com
- Amazon,ca
- Goodreads